MASTERING E-COMMERCE

INCREASING PROFITS AND
DOMINATING THE ONLINE
MARKETPLACE

CHARLES WEALTH

About Author

Mastering e-Commerce teaches you how to leverage the power of the niche brand model in Mastering E-Commerce. It is jam-packed with helpful information and valuable advice, including guidance on creating new goods from conception to launch and beyond, management and goal-setting strategies, and tried-and-true online marketing tactics.

"Mastering E-Commerce" servers as your ultimate guide to achieving entrepreneurial success, If you're sick of making it through each day and want to succeed in the world of online business. Discover the fascinating world of e-Commerce and get the skills necessary to successfully market your digital items.

This book gives you the tools you need for success by giving you an immersive experience within a virtual toolbox rather than just giving you a glimpse of it.

Your route to online success will become stronger with each new attempt, making you an unstoppable power in the digital jungle.

I'm Charles Wealth, a seasoned e-commerce professional who has a love for assisting companies to prosper in the online market, having been active in the e-commerce sector for more than 20 years.

I started as an e-commerce consultant as people began to recognize my ability over time. In order to help many firms and entrepreneurs manage the constantly changing e-commerce industry, I have produced and created several online e-commerce resources and courses over the years with a passion to help online entrepreneurs become success stories.

My main educational tenets center on experiential learning and keeping up with current market developments. For startups and established businesses, I have led countless numbers of seminars, webinars, and training sessions to help entrepreneurs improve their online presence, boost sales, and increase profitability.

I have made significant contributions to top e-commerce platforms throughout the years, assisting companies in reaching their target markets. I'm an expert at producing compelling product descriptions, material that is optimized for search engines, and sales copy that turns browsers into customers.

I've written insightful articles, eBooks, and guides as a thought leader in the field of e-commerce writing, sharing my knowledge on subjects including content marketing tactics, e-commerce best practices, and current market trends.

Beyond my writing skills, I am renowned for my commitment to keeping up with the constantly changing e-commerce market. This book focuses on assisting companies and individuals in thriving in the digital market by supplying content that connects with customers and stimulates commerce.

Table of Contents

Using data analytics to track the success of your online store

Chapter 15
Encourage client feedback and gather it to make required adjustments and foster confidence

Chapter 16
Adding new markets and product lines

Chapter 17
Keep up with business changes and technological developments

Chapter 1

E-Commerce: What is it?

E-commerce, short for electronic commerce, refers to the buying and selling of goods and services over the internet or through electronic means. It involves online transactions and the exchange of products or services between businesses, consumers, or a combination of both.

E-commerce can encompass a wide range of activities, including online retail stores, digital marketplaces, electronic payments, and online auctions. It has become a fundamental part of the modern economy, providing convenience and access to a global marketplace for both businesses and consumers.

The term "e-commerce," which stands for "electrical commerce," describes the exchange of products and services through the internet or by other electronic means. It entails online transactions and the trade of goods or services between companies, clients, or a mix of both.

Online retail establishments, digital marketplaces, electronic payments, and online auctions are just a few examples of the diverse activities that can be included in e-commerce. It now forms a crucial component of the contemporary economy, giving consumers and businesses convenience and access to a global market.

Chapter 2

Recognizing your target market's requirements, preferences, niche, and prospective rivals

Knowing your target market enables you to accurately cater for your marketing efforts to their needs and interests. By doing this, it is more likely to connect with and resonate with potential clients. Developing goods or services that are more likely to be purchased requires an understanding of the needs of your target market. You can develop products and services that specifically address their needs and wants.

Customer loyalty and sales may rise If your website, user interface, and entire purchasing experience are tailored to the preferences of your audience. You can find market gaps or areas where you can surpass your competition by researching them. It enables you to stand out from the competition and provide your customers something special.

You may set competitive and profitable prices for your goods or services by taking into account the pricing strategies of your rivals and the purchasing power of your target market. Knowing what subjects or goods your audience is interested in will help you engage them more successfully on social media, through email marketing, and through other means.

Customer loyalty is increased and repeat business is promoted by continually exceeding your audience's expectations and providing value. Understanding your audience will help you modify your business plan in response to shifting consumer preferences and market trends.

Making informed judgments, customizing your business tactics, and ultimately succeeding in the fiercely competitive e-commerce sector require a thorough awareness of your target audience and the competitive landscape.

Chapter 3

A thorough business plan, a budget, a strategy, and an original value proposition

An e-commerce business can be considerably boosted in a number of ways by having a thorough business plan, clearly defined goals, a well-thought-out budget, and a clear strategy. Your e-commerce venture has a roadmap thanks to your business strategy. It explains your vision, mission, and particular goals and aids in keeping you concentrated on your goals.

Utilizing a budget guarantees efficient resource allocation. It aids in cost management, investment planning, and making sure you have the resources needed to run and expand your e-commerce firm. You can decide on product offerings, marketing avenues, and consumer segmentation with the use of a strategy. Better results and more efficient use of resources may result from this.

You stand out from rivals because of your distinctive value proposition. It provides a response to the query, "Why should customers choose you?" In a competitive e-commerce market, a great value proposition may draw in and keep customers. A marketing strategy ought to be part of your approach. You may efficiently reach your target audience with a well-crafted plan through a variety of channels, including social media, SEO, email marketing, and paid advertising.

Tactics for interacting with and fostering consumer connections can be part of a clear strategy. This can entail tailored recommendations, reward programs, and top-notch customer support.

A thorough plan enables you to scale your firm when possibilities present themselves and adjust to shifting market conditions. It offers a structure for development and enlargement.
A strong business plan might inspire trust in investors or lenders if you're looking for outside capital. It shows that you have a methodical strategy for success.

You should include potential risks and contingencies in your plan. Being ready for obstacles can make you traverse them more successfully. Your plan's goals should be detailed and measurable so that you can keep tabs on your development. With this data-driven methodology, you may change as necessary.

Building a solid foundation for success in the e-commerce industry requires a thorough business plan, specific goals, budgeting, and a well-defined strategy. They offer guidance, command over finances, and a competitive edge that can result in higher sales, enduring client loyalty, and long-term success.

Chapter 4

E-commerce rules and laws

Almost always is an excellent moment to launch an online store. Because of the globalization of the internet and the accessibility of technologies like Shopify, anyone can establish a business, regardless of technical proficiency.

But there are some complicated legal considerations when selling online. Knowing which laws apply to you is essential because they vary depending on the nation and state. Laws governing e-commerce are also dynamic and flexible. You need to keep informed in order to be able to defend yourself and your company in order to benefit from a prosperous online store,

Running your shop properly requires you to be aware of and compliant with the laws that are relevant to you as an online company owner. Understanding e-commerce regulations is crucial for preserving your brand, your assets, and your ability to keep your customers happy.

Ideal e-commerce rules safeguard both consumers and corporations. Some laws support identity theft prevention, fraud case mitigation, and data privacy in general.

Additionally, similar regulations are occasionally implemented to safeguard consumers from companies. For instance, rules exist to forbid collecting data from children, as well as engaging in deceptive or inaccurate advertising activities. Even when a company has access to a customer's payment information, executing unlawful transactions is prohibited by law.

You want to take precautions for your company just as it's necessary to protect your customers. The right of a company to conduct business honestly is protected by numerous laws. To safeguard intellectual property and ideas, for instance, trademark, patent, and copyright laws are in place.

Knowing the tax regulations, such as those pertaining to sales tax, import charges, and annual files, safeguards your assets. Understanding employment and labor regulations will also help you prevent negative consequences for violations and guarantee that you're treating your employees fairly.

We work in a data-driven sector, so it's crucial to ensure that you're gathering and storing data legally. Some crucial points to bear in mind are:

Website monitoring Despite the fact that there is no federal legislation requiring US online retailers to track website user data in a specific way, some states do have regulations of this nature.

The California Consumer Privacy Act (CCPA), for instance, is one of the harshest regulations.

According to this law, retailers must grant customers the right to know what information is being gathered about them and how it will be used, to have that information deleted, to opt out of having it shared or sold, and to be treated equally when exercising these rights. To find out whether laws apply, check your state or states. If you sell internationally, check out the <u>European Union's General Data Protection Regulation (GDPR)</u>.

Email marketing: To reduce unsolicited and spam emails, the Federal Trade Commission (FTC) approved the Controlling the Assault of Non-Solicited Pornography and Marketing Act (CAN-SPAM). The law mandates that companies send truthful and transparent emails, refrain from misleading recipients, include their business address, provide an opt-out option and abide by recipients' demands, and keep an eye on any email marketing activities carried out by third parties.

Privacy regulations: The Federal Communication Commission (FCC) has demanded that online firms provide users with privacy policies that describe how they utilize their data. The FTC also mandates that all retailers adhere to the conditions outlined in their privacy policies. Most states additionally have extra privacy laws of their own.

The Children's Online Privacy Protection Act (COPPA) of the FTC forbids companies from tracking information from or about children under the age of 13 and from falsely advertising to them. This is something that retailers who sell children's products will want to focus on more.

The Health Breach Notification Rule may be of interest to online retailers in the health and wellness sector. If you experience a data breach, you could be compelled to notify your customers if you have any information about them that relates to their health.

A written Identity Theft Prevention Program that outlines the actions to follow to identify and resolve suspected incidents of identity theft is also required by the Red Flags Rule for enterprises.

Chapter 5

12 Guidelines for Picking the Best E-Commerce Platforms

1. Hosting and Platform ownership

E-Commerce platforms are professionals at framing and communicating their offerings as you promote your goods and services. With over 370 eCommerce solutions available globally, choosing the ideal eCommerce platform for your company can be challenging. Of course, you could also determine that a specially created solution is the best.

In order to engage customers with the brand, you must first control your cost-to-sales ratio. Additionally, you must make sure that the staff is fully supported in putting sales and marketing ideas into practice.

You may get a better sense of the things to think about when making sure that your eCommerce platform is among the best by reading the text that follows. While doing so, there are a few questions you might ask yourself about particular features.

1. Ownership of the hosting and platform

Platforms for online sales might be cloud-based or self-hosted. In the former, you are responsible for finding the hosting, handling the installation, and managing the updates. This might occasionally get pricey. Better security management and more control over the internet platform are benefits. Additionally, your data is more clearly visible.

You can obtain hosting for a cloud-hosted platform through services like AWS (Amazon Web Services), indicating that the cloud platform controls the brand uptime. You will have less control over the servers, but the expenses are lower and the customer support is better. The server cannot be customized to meet your unique requirements.

You can choose between Open-Source, SaaS, or Headless platforms in terms of platform ownership.

You can have better control and ownership with open-source systems (like WooCommerce and Magento), as the source code is not just available but also modifiable. You would be in charge of analytics, web hosting, security problems, and integrations (with things like CRM, CMS, or ESP). These kinds of platforms are preferred by firms with an IT or development focus.

You cannot, however, change features through updating or any other means. Additionally, they might grow excessively complicated and expensive to operate. They require far too much technical expertise.

Delivering an omnichannel experience that engages customers wherever they are, whenever they want to shop, is simple with the top eCommerce platforms. This gives your company a competitive edge and aids in increasing client trust. Headless Commerce offers a quicker time to market while also significantly lowering costs.

2. Ownership Cost

One of the first factors to take into account when evaluating each eCommerce platform is pricing. You need to be aware of the whole cost of each platform, whether you're a tiny firm just starting or an established brick-and-mortar store coming online.

There will almost always be a monthly subscription for platforms. With each platform, transaction fees are also included. When making decisions, you must take both the up-front and ongoing expenditures into account. Don't give up essential items in exchange for a cheaper price. To get the best value for your money, weigh the advantages and disadvantages.

As a last step in determining opportunity costs, think about how your customers will pay for your products. For instance, certain platforms don't support payment through external suppliers (like PayPal). This can be a huge inconvenience for your customers — a frustration that can lead to shopping cart abandonment.

3. Integrations

When determining if your platform is among the finest eCommerce platforms, integrations and plugins are additional important considerations. Not all systems support every integration, so make sure you comprehend your business needs before evaluating the features and functions that are offered. The most popular plugins to seek for are listed below:

- Accounting: Delivers financial data, such as sales, taxes, revenues, and profits.

- Email marketing: gives you the ability to communicate with your customers.

- Customers loyalty programs: can be rewarded for utilizing your products and making additional purchases through customer loyalty programs.

- Payment and Shipping: You may now process payments and ship goods with ease and accuracy.
- Third Party Digital Tools: Easy integration with technologies like marketing automation systems, CRMs, and ERPs is made possible by third-party digital solutions.

4. User Experience (UX) & Themes

Who comes to mind when you think about the most well-known digital businesses? Airbnb? Lyft? Netflix? They strive to provide a fantastic, intuitive UX with their elegant minimalism, warm interfaces, and wide range of options.

According to research, a brand's quality of user experience will surpass both price and product as a crucial differentiator by the year 2020. Consumers of today prefer to shop in interesting, immersive places rather than just buying goods.

The style of your online store is determined by a theme, and the majority of eCommerce systems provide a choice of possibilities. Some themes come with the subscription for free, while others are premium and cost extra to use. To differentiate yourself from the competition, it's worth the cost.
, as a user-friendly experience is essential to converting surfers into customers.

5. eCommerce Platform Scalability and Speed

Your platform must provide a lightning-fast experience in the era of "Micro-moments," which Google defines as "an intent-rich moment when a person turns to a device to act on a need to know, go, do, or buy." And when you scale and expand the business, this has to stay the same. Choose a platform that expands together with your company to be among the finest platforms for eCommerce.

While assessing the performance and scalability of a platform is not straightforward, you can look at the areas that might be problematic, such as slow load times, frozen pages, 404 errors, and other poor performance indications. knowing the maximum number of users the platform can accommodate at A crucial component of your study is looking at typical site speed and peak traffic periods to see how it scales both horizontally and vertically.

Our recommendation is to look for a cloud-hosted, scalable solution with pre-built features and functionalities that immediately meet the demands of your expanding organization. It's also important to take into account things like sophisticated caching techniques and the capacity to automatically delete content when product descriptions need to be updated. Make sure your users get good technical and customer support as well.

Immediately: How does the platform handle scaling?
What does the delay look like when you update?

Can you refresh your shop when it's busy?

6. Product management system (store functionality and ease of use)

The Product Management System is essential to the operation of your company. To provide an engaging purchasing experience, today's admins require advanced eCommerce product management right out of the box.

It's critical to take into account features and functions like bulk product upload (using CSV or Excel files), categorization, advanced features (such as wish lists, product comparisons, and recently viewed products), shipping options, and dynamic filters (such as sorting, price range, color, size, location, etc.) when evaluating store functionality to create the best eCommerce platforms. The admin will have more opportunity to maximize revenue the more control they have over designing a strong, dynamic store.

Simple Questions:
Can you easily map things to various categories you create?
Can you link different delivery options to specific products on the platform?
Can high-resolution product photos be bulk uploaded?

Can you make product combinations and variations based on factors like size, color, and so on?

7. eCommerce Platform Security In the digital world, website security issues are crucial.

In addition to the fact that there are strict international regulations safeguarding consumer privacy, a security breach can harm one of your most important assets: trust.

Security problems aren't your fault, although they do happen frequently. Identity theft (71%), phishing (66%), and account theft (63%) are the three most common types of online eCommerce crimes, according to a recent survey. And according to our research, security worries in the IT and entertainment sectors are more serious than those related to digital vision and strategy, at 51% and 44%, respectively.

You must carefully assess the security credentials of the eCommerce platform you're evaluating for your current demands and future expansion because you're handling so much sensitive data. All give some level of protection by default, but many also provide additional security features like fraud protection and DDoS monitoring. Owners of online stores should take special care to guarantee PCI compliance, SSL, and safe data backups.

Additionally, confirm that the platform you choose complies with PCI standards. These specifications guarantee that businesses that process or send credit card information do so in a secure setting. For instance, we hold the highest level of accreditation for a service provider, PCI DSS Level 1 certification. This level of dedication from a provider denotes dedication to your data and security.

8. Support for Multiple Payment Gateways

Customers can pay for your goods and services in a variety of ways, and the process is straightforward. This calls for a connection between your store and a trustworthy, secure eCommerce payment gateway – a specialized processor that securely transfers money from your customers' bank accounts into their own. Although it might seem obvious, not all eCommerce platforms are compatible with all payment gateways. Geographical considerations are vital; localizing the payment procedure is important.

Even while eWallets are expanding significantly on a global scale, they still do not dominate the payments industry. Therefore, be sure that the platform you select offers you a sufficient range of payment methods to appease your core clientele. Our study on 8. Support for Multiple Payment Gateways
Customers can pay for your goods and services in a variety of ways, and the process is straightforward.

This calls for a connection between your store and a trustworthy, secure eCommerce payment gateway – a specialized processor that securely transfers money from your customers' bank accounts into their own. Although it might seem obvious, not all eCommerce platforms are compatible with all payment gateways. Geographical considerations are vital; localizing the payment procedure is important.

Even while eWallets are expanding significantly on a global scale, they still do not dominate the payments industry. Therefore, be sure that the platform you select offers you a sufficient range of payment methods to appease your core clientele.

9. Personalization

You may provide your online customers with a customized experience that puts your site beyond all others thanks to machine learning and AI. The finest eCommerce platforms have a recommendation engine that dynamically suggests products to customers based on standards like:

Demographics: location, age, sex, etc.
Psychographics: lifestyle, personality, and interests
Context includes things like location, time of day, type of device, and weather.

Items that have recently been seen, active searches, and items in abandoned carts

History: Previous purchases, correspondence from back when you were an email member
The platform may provide a real-time tailored experience to the customer by taking into account a variety of data factors.

10. Mobile compatibility

Merchants are increasingly considering mobile payment options since digital communication and transactions through mobile devices are expected to reach $432.24 billion in the US by 2022. You may provide your online customers with a customized experience that puts your site beyond all others thanks to machine learning and AI. The finest eCommerce platforms have a recommendation engine that dynamically suggests products to customers based on standards like:

Demographics: location, age, sex, etc.
Psychographics: lifestyle, personality, and interests

Context includes things like location, time of day, type of device, and weather. Items that have recently been seen, active searches, and items in abandoned carts. Previous purchases, correspondence from back when you were an email member

The platform may provide a real-time tailored experience to the customer by taking into account a variety of data factors. merchants are increasingly looking at platforms that provide a mobile-ready experience for their online stores.

Particularly in our post-pandemic era is this true. Nowadays, a sizable amount of internet purchases, including those for groceries, home items, prescription drugs, and other necessities, are made on smartphones. The greatest eCommerce platforms will create a framework for a user-friendly, seamless customer journey. A well-designed mobile experience is essential from start to finish, including the design, navigation, layout, and overall user experience.

Additionally, the company must be able to sell goods and services via a variety of platforms, including Facebook, Instagram, Amazon, and others.

10. Friendliness for SEO

The success of your store depends on search engine optimization (SEO), and the top eCommerce platforms will construct their architecture taking SEO into account. Building organic SEO takes time, and Particularly in our post-pandemic era is this true. Nowadays, a sizable amount of internet purchases, including those for groceries, home items, prescription drugs, and other necessities, are made on smartphones. The greatest eCommerce platforms will create a framework for a user-friendly, seamless customer journey. A well-designed mobile experience is essential from start to finish, including the design, navigation, layout, and overall user experience.

Additionally, the company must be able to sell goods and services via a variety of platforms, including Facebook, Instagram, Amazon, and others.

11. Friendliness for SEO

The success of your store depends on search engine optimization (SEO), and the top eCommerce platforms will construct their architecture taking SEO into account. Building organic SEO takes time, but it is made much simpler when the platform you use is created with best practices in mind and prioritizes staying up to date with Google's algorithm updates.

When it comes to SEO, not all eCommerce platforms are made equal. You must determine whether SEO tools are supported, from basic functions like changing metadata (tags, descriptions), captioning, and describing images, to more complex ones like adding canonical tags and pagination in product search results.

Quick Questions: Is it possible to add a unique domain name?
- Can you add a custom domain name?
- Do you have access to the robot.txt file of the platform?

- Does the platform allow you to convert into SEO-friendly URL structures?
- Do you have access to update the XML sitemap?
- Can you integrate Google Analytics

12. Order Management System

Your eCommerce experience must be easy and quick to place orders. According to research, more than 80% of online buyers anticipate regular updates on their orders. This means that if you want to compete, you must have an OMS that makes the process accurate, visible, and interactive.

You can be sure that purchases are executed accurately and on schedule thanks to features like order tracking, email notifications, and shipping service API.

In order for customers to be confident that things are in-stock and prepared for shipping, there must be seamless communication between your OMS and Inventory Management System (IMS). ERP and CRM applications can be integrated using APIs or installed as plugins, among other important connectors.

Simple Questions:

- How does the OMS aid in the accomplishment of your corporate goals?
- Can the OMS support international eCommerce orders?
- Does the OMS continually update based on evolving customer desires or needs?
- Does the OMS support inventory visibility and streamlined ordering from suppliers?

Examples of the top eCommerce platforms

It's challenging to select the best eCommerce platforms because you need to consider a number of factors. The best option will match your needs in terms of functionality, price, features, and security. Despite the fact that facets may vary in terms of more or less in various systems.

According to Statista, the share of eCommerce platforms as of April 2021 was as follows. Later, in 2022, Forbes Advisor proposed a logical comparison of the several platforms. This analysis is beneficial and will aid a potential user. Pricing, features & functionality, usability, inventory management, and multichannel selling comprise the approach of this analysis:

The Best eCommerce Sites of 2023

Amazon → The world's leader in B2C retail

eBay → The best C2C marketplace

AliExpress → Offers the cheap prices

Walmart → Unlimited assortment of your products

Rakuten → Referral and cashback programs

Wildberries → Popular in Russia, known for a wide range of clothing and household items

Ozon → Russia's answer to Amazon, offers a broad assortment of goods.

Flipkart → Private Indian eCommerce company

Samsung → The world's leader in electronics and media sales

Etsy → Specializes in handmade, vintage, and unique goods

Others are:

Square Online: Best for Omnichannel Selling.

BigCommerce: Best for Boosting Sales.

Weebly: Best Value.

Squarespace: Best for Beginners.

Ecwid: Best for no Transaction Fees.

WooCommerce: Best Free WordPress Plugin.

CoreCommerce: Best for Pre Existing Websites.

Slar platform Semrush. After the list, let's look into each eCommerce site to understand its importance etc.

Chapter 6

Advice on how to source your products.

Imagine you have a fantastic idea for a brand-new online store. Or perhaps you've found a brand-new product that would be a great addition to your present line. How to go about getting the products you need to sell your idea is one of the first things you'll need to decide. We'll examine several sorts of product sourcing, the best product sourcing tactics, and product sourcing techniques in this article.

How does product sourcing work?

Finding reliable market vendors from whom you can purchase high-quality goods is the main goal of product sourcing. You might require parts to manufacture your product, or you might just want to resell it. Obviously, getting the highest-quality item at the best price is the ultimate objective. Your firms' growth will be fueled in part by that profit margin.

Of course, finding products isn't always as simple as it seems. It necessitates selecting a plan for product procurement and doing some research to guarantee you identify a reputable vendor (and

possibly a few backups, but more on that later). So let's get
started!

3 Methods of Choosing Products:

So, as a new eCommerce company, how do you source a
product? There are essentially three possibilities to think about:
self-made goods or services, collaboration with a producer or
distributor, or association with a fulfillment facility. Some of the
factors for each are listed below.

1. Self-made goods or services

While the sale of handcrafted goods, such as woodworking crafts,
knitted blankets, jewelry made by hand, and paintings created by
hand, was formerly restricted to flea markets and similar venues,
you can now do so online. You will nevertheless want resources.
You might get these from specialty shops, large merchants, estate
sales, and other places. After that, you must decide how to ship
orders. This will definitely require visits to the UPS, FedEx, or
USPS store as a starter. However, when your business grows, you
might need to think about using a shipping service to save time
and money so that you can focus your efforts on creating new
items and promoting your brand.

2. Cooperating with a Wholesaler or Manufacturer

You may decide it's time to work with a manufacturer or wholesaler to develop your product when your company grows and you realize you don't have the time or resources to build all of your products yourself, or at the very least to augment DIY efforts during peak seasons. You'll need to locate the products if you choose this course of action; a reliable manufacturer or wholesaler can probably provide you some possibilities.

Naturally, you'll want to thoroughly investigate possible partners to make sure you're hiring someone who is reputable, trustworthy, and economical. Their customer service assistance, delivery schedules, and any requirements for a minimum quantity are further factors.

3. Employing a fulfillment facility

You can buy from a vendor and sell their products on your online store by using a fulfillment center, often known as a third-party logistics (3PL) provider or dropshipper. Inventory, packing, and order fulfillment are basically unloaded! You should still investigate possible fulfillment partners to make sure you're working with a trustworthy and ethical company, just like you would with any manufacturer or wholesaler. See more information about the benefits of a fulfillment center here.

10. Product Sourcing Techniques

There are several things to think about while sourcing products. We'll walk you through our list of the ten best methods for finding products to help your business succeed.

- Constantly Be Sourcing
- **Do Your Homework**
- **Follow the Leader**
- **Take the Lead**
- Get Offline
- **Look Local**
- **Cut Out Middle Men**
- **Reconsider Bulk Buying**
- **Know Your Supplier**
- **Have a Plan B**

By continuing to look at new products and market trends, you can remain relevant to consumers and maintain profitability. you want to be sure products fit within your product portfolio. Oddball products that are unrelated to your flagship products are likely to confuse your buyers. There's no shame in following other successful sellers' business models to be successful yourself. So, go ahead and order a product from one of your competitors. You will likely be able to find out who sourced the product by checking the packaging.

In some cases, it may be best to branch out on your own and set your own product trends after conducting some research and speaking with suppliers. You may be able to find a great product source by visiting trade shows. At these events, you can also meet product manufacturers and developers first-hand, establishing a real one-on-one relationship that could last for years.

To increase profit margins, a lot of eCommerce sellers will look overseas, often to China, for manufacturing help. However, sometimes it may be in your best interest to keep product sourcing and manufacturing a bit closer to home. The more businesses involved in your supply chain, the higher the price you'll pay for a product. So, when possible, go directly to the source for your products.

Buying in bulk will almost always get you a better price, but if the product is not a fast seller, you could be tied down with inventory for a long time. And, if a newer model comes out, your inventory could become essentially worthless. That loss can really hurt your bottom line.

Nurture your supplier relationship so that you're first on their call list when they have a hot new product and you're first in line when you've encountered a product default and need it corrected.

Having a backup supplier is simply a smart move, and it doesn't always mean it's because you don't trust your primary supplier. What if there's a disaster that impacts your primary supplier, such as a data breach, a major storm, or a product recall? This can completely upend your supply chain through no fault of your own.

Chapter 7

*Secure payment gateways and mobile-friendly
ecommerce optimization*

For any e-commerce business, it's important to find an affordable,
secure payment gateway that integrates with your site. However,
there are so many options available. Fortunately, finding the right
gateway is easier when you know what to look for.

In this post, we'll take a closer look at payment gateways and
discuss some key factors to consider. Then, we'll explore five of
the best payment gateways for e-commerce businesses. Let's get
started!

Finding an affordable, secure payment gateway that interfaces
with your website is crucial for every e-commerce firm. There are,
however, a lot of choices. Fortunately, when you know what to look
for, finding the appropriate gateway is simpler.

In this article, we'll examine payment gateways in more detail and
go over some important things to think about. Below are:

The 10 best payment solutions for eCommerce and others:

- **Amazon Pay (Recommended)**
- **Paycomet (Recommended)**
- Worldline
- Worldpay
- Stripe
- Paypal
- Redsys
- Adyen
- Shopify Payments
- Checkout.com
- Addon Payments
- Braintree
- Hipay
- Kevin
- Kushki
- Lyra Network
- Mangopay
- Monei
- Multisafepay
- MyPOS
- Neopay
- Neteller
- Paylands
- PayRetailers
- Payxpert
- Shift 4 (ex SecurionPay)
- Simplify

- SiPay
- Sprinque
- Storeden
- Swipe
- UniversalPay

Chapter 8

Exceptional product listings, pictures, and descriptions

Customers are helped to comprehend the product better by concise, well-written descriptions and high-resolution photographs. This lessens ambiguity and raises the possibility that a purchase will be made. A better overall buying experience is made possible by high-quality listings, making it more pleasurable and user-friendly. Increased client satisfaction and recurring business may result from this.

Customers are more likely to trust product listings that are expert and accurate. Customers are more inclined to trust that a seller is credible and reliable when they see thorough descriptions and crisp photographs. The likelihood that buyers would receive a product that falls short of their expectations is decreased by accurate product descriptions and photos. This can therefore result in fewer returns and exchanges, saving the e-commerce company time and money.

A website's search engine rating can be raised by having properly optimized product listings. This means that in addition to drawing in more customers, high-quality listings also make it simpler for potential buyers to discover the products in the first place. Superior listings can give a business a competitive edge in a crowded e-commerce sector. Customers are more likely to select a product that has comprehensive information and eye-catching graphics than one that is poorly presented.

A strong brand image is enhanced by high-quality listings. Customers may become devoted to your brand and spread the word about it when they associate it with precision, professionalism, and attention to detail. In-depth descriptions can also be used to emphasize the characteristics and advantages of a product, enabling successful cross-selling and upselling that can raise the average order value.

High-quality photographs and succinct descriptions are essential for delivering a positive mobile shopping experience as more consumers purchase on mobile devices. Listings that are mobile-friendly can help you reach this expanding market of buyers. As a last point, investing in top-notch product listings, photos, and descriptions is crucial for the success of e-commerce. Along with aiding in customer acquisition and retention, it also improves the company's general standing and bottom line.

Chapter 9

Effective inventory management system to prevent overstocking or understocking

Maintaining the ideal balance between overstocking and understocking is made possible by optimized stock levels. Understocking results in lost sales while overstocking consumes resources and storage space. When inventories are managed properly, products are always available when needed without being overstocked. Online shoppers anticipate prompt deliveries. Effective inventory management guarantees that goods are available and can be transported quickly, increasing customer satisfaction and encouraging repeat business.

E-commerce companies can reduce storage expenses and the chance of products going out of date by avoiding overstocking. They can also benefit from sales on popular items when buying in bulk. To accurately estimate demand, inventory systems can examine previous sales data and consumer behavior. This enables companies to prepare for seasonal changes and modify their product offerings accordingly.

Customers may turn elsewhere if there are frequently out-of-stock situations as a result of understocking. By setting off reorder points and automating replenishment procedures, a good system helps to avoid this. Less capital is tied up in surplus goods thanks to effective inventory management. This frees up money that may be used to fund the development of new products or other areas of the company.

Inventory management systems frequently connect with order processing and shipping as well as other areas of the online store. Operations are streamlined by this integration, which lowers errors and boosts productivity. Systems for managing inventories offer useful information on a variety of topics, including product performance and supplier dependability. This information can help with strategic decisions about choosing a product, setting a price, and sourcing. In conclusion, efficient inventory tracking and management are crucial for e-commerce enterprises to develop and profitably, stay competitive, cut expenses, and exceed customer expectations.

Chapter 10

Marketing plan using content marketing, paid advertising, social media marketing, and email marketing

An e-commerce company can benefit significantly from implementing a comprehensive marketing plan that combines social media marketing, email marketing, paid advertising, and content marketing. Each element's potential impact on e-commerce is listed below:

Social media platforms have a large audience that e-commerce companies may use to boost brand recognition and visibility among their target market.
Through direct messaging, comments, likes, and other forms of interaction, social media encourages client engagement. Creating a vibrant online community can increase client trust and loyalty.

Online retailers can highlight their goods via aesthetically engaging posts, tales, and videos. For promoting products, websites like Instagram and Pinterest are very useful. Customers can give direct comments and evaluations via social media, which can be helpful for enhancing goods and services.

By delivering individualized product recommendations, incentives, and updates, email marketing enables firms to cultivate relationships with current customers. Email can be used by e-commerce companies to remind customers of abandoned shopping carts and persuade them to finish their purchases.

Through email marketing, businesses may deliver tailored content and offers by segmenting their email lists based on customer behavior, demographics, and preferences. Businesses can target certain demographics, interests, and behaviors using paid advertising on websites like Google adverts and Facebook Ads to make sure their adverts are seen by the proper population.

Paid advertising is an effective technique for e-commerce enterprises looking for quick results because it may swiftly drive traffic and sales. Businesses have control over their advertising spending because of the ability to define budgets and bid tactics.

Content marketing, such as blog posts, videos, and guides, can educate and inform customers about products, helping them make informed purchasing decisions. High-quality content can improve search engine rankings, increasing organic traffic to the e-commerce website. Consistent and valuable content builds brand authority and trust, making customers more likely to choose the e-commerce site over competitors.

A well-rounded marketing strategy that combines these elements can drive traffic, engagement, and conversions for an e-commerce business. Each component serves a specific purpose in reaching and engaging with the target audience, building brand loyalty, and ultimately driving sales and revenue growth. Successful e-commerce businesses often integrate these marketing tactics into a cohesive and data-driven strategy to maximize their impact.

Customers can learn more about items and make informed selections by using content marketing tools like blog articles, videos, and guides. High-quality content can raise a website's search engine ranks and boost organic traffic. Consumers are more likely to prefer the e-commerce site over rivals when there is consistent and valuable content since it increases brand authority and confidence.

For an e-commerce business, a well-rounded marketing strategy that incorporates these components can increase traffic, engagement, and conversions. Each element has a specific function that helps reach and interact with the target audience, foster brand loyalty, and ultimately boost sales and revenue. To optimize their influence, profitable e-commerce companies frequently combine these marketing techniques into a unified and data-driven approach.

Chapter 11

Six Ways on how to Create a Responsive Support System with Simple Return Procedures

An e-commerce company's profitability and reputation can be significantly impacted by responsive service and simple return procedures. These elements' effects on e-Commerce in the following 6 ways:

1. Responsive support fosters pleasure and trust. Customers can receive prompt assistance when they run into problems or have inquiries, resulting in a great purchasing experience. When things don't live up to expectations, customers are less irritated by return procedures that are made simple. This raises satisfaction and promotes customer loyalty.

2. A reputation for providing exceptional customer service might provide you a competitive edge. Positive online evaluations and word-of-mouth recommendations can help draw in new clients. Customers are more likely to perceive companies favorably and to view them as reliable and customer-focused if they have easy return policies.

3. If customers can't get rapid support, they may abandon their carts if they run into problems during the checkout process or have

queries about a product. Support that responds quickly can reduce cart abandonment. Some buyers may feel less hesitant while making online purchases if they know they can simply return products if they change their minds.

4. Excellent customer service
encourages repeat business. Customers are more inclined to make subsequent purchases when they feel appreciated and supported. Customers may feel more secure in their purchase choices and are therefore more likely to visit the e-commerce site again if the return process is simple.

5. Responsive customer service can help a company stand out from rivals in a congested e-commerce sector. It's a strategy for standing out by offering great service. Offering simpler and more forgiving return policies than rivals can draw clients who appreciate ease and flexibility.

6. The e-commerce company can save time and money by providing effective help to customers before their complaints or chargebacks become formal. Customers are less likely to dispute charges with their credit card issuers when they have simple return choices.

A great customer experience is essential for the long-term survival of an e-commerce business, and is facilitated through responsive support and simple return procedures. They increase consumer satisfaction, strengthen brand reputation, lower cart abandonment, promote repeat business, and provide businesses an edge over their competitors.

Chapter 12

Various payment options

Multiple payment options can significantly affect e-commerce in a number of different ways. Giving customers a choice of payment methods satisfies their wide range of preferences. Credit cards, PayPal, and digital wallets like Apple Pay or Google Pay may all be preferred by different people. By offering a variety of options, you lower purchasing barriers and improve user experience.

The recommended payment options vary by area. For instance, alternative payment systems like Alipay and WeChat Pay are popular in China, whereas credit cards are popular in the US. E-commerce companies can more successfully enter overseas markets by catering to these interests.

Limited options for payment are a frequent cause of cart abandonment. Customers are more likely to abandon their purchase if they are unable to pay how they choose. Several payment options can help reduce cart abandonment rates.

Payment method variety can improve security. Some techniques, such as tokenized mobile payments, can provide additional security measures. Customers who are concerned about the security of their financial information may find this reassuring. Some clients might not have access to credit cards or conventional banking services. These underdeveloped markets may become accessible to online shopping through the use of alternative payment mechanisms like prepaid cards or digital wallets.

The transaction fees associated with various payment methods vary. E-commerce enterprises may be able to reduce their overall payment processing expenses by providing a variety of options. Multiple payment options can offer insightful data. Marketing and company tactics can be influenced by knowing which techniques are most popular with your customers.

Providing a variety of payment alternatives can give you a competitive edge. It might distinguish your online store from rivals who just provide a few options. The administrative and technical challenges of integrating numerous payment methods, such as security compliance and customer assistance, must be taken into account. Additionally, not every payment option may be appropriate for every business, so it's important to know your industry and target audience before choosing which options to provide.

Chapter 13

Improving the effectiveness and efficiency of the delivery procedure

There are numerous strategies to save shipping expenses and enhance delivery processes. Strategic Planning, Logistics Optimization, Increasing Efficiency, and Shipping Terms and Policy are the four categories we've divided up our amazing shipping and e-commerce business techniques into.

Planning Strategically

Effective shipping cost reduction starts with strategic planning. It entails reviewing your shipping procedures, seeking out areas for improvement, and putting ideas into practice that support your corporate objectives. The following are the essential elements of a strategic plan to lower transportation costs:

1. Analysis of shipping volume

It's crucial to analyze the shipping data already in existence in order to comprehend your shipping volume trends before you start implementing any approaches. To find any trends in peak seasons, order frequency, or shipping locations, analyze historical shipping data.

Based on your real shipping volume, this study will assist you in negotiating better costs with shipping carriers. For instance, during the holiday season, a gourmet food and bakery online company would experience a spike in shipment. With this knowledge, they can bargain with carriers in advance to get good rates for this busy time.

If you're a supplier who frequently receives orders from a business client, you might be able to combine several orders into a single shipment to save the cost of sending each order individually.

2. Zone improvement

In order to optimize your zone distribution, you must group your shipment destinations according to how close they are to your warehouse. You can reduce shipping expenses by carefully choosing shipping companies based on the delivery zone.

For instance, local delivery services can be used for close-by zones if you run an online clothes company with consumers spread out across the nation. By choosing national carriers for far-off zones, this brings down the shipping distances and costs for these orders while ensuring effective long-distance delivery.

3. Zone optimization

It involves dividing your shipment destinations into areas according to how close they are to your warehouse. You can reduce shipping expenses by carefully choosing shipping companies based on the delivery zone.

For instance, local delivery services can be used for close-by zones if you run an online clothes company with consumers spread out across the nation. By choosing national carriers for far-off zones, this brings down the shipping distances and costs for these orders while ensuring effective long-distance delivery.

4. Calculating the weight of dimensions

Pricing based on dimensional weight takes into account a package's size in relation to its actual weight. To prevent paying for empty space, packaging must be optimized. Consider that you offer pillows at your online home goods store. Due to cushions' mass, traditional packaging may result in exorbitant dimensional weight charges. Vacuum-sealed packaging, on the other hand, allows you to dramatically reduce package size while also reducing dimensional weight and, in turn, transportation expenses.

5. Prepaid delivery

Prepaid shipping entails paying for a predetermined quantity of shipping labels in advance at a reduced price. If your delivery volume is consistent, this is advantageous. You can get better rates by prepaying for the shipping label as opposed to paying for each shipment separately. The subscription box providers frequently employ this technique. Prepaid shipping labels, for instance, can be advantageous for a gourmet snack subscription box because of the regularity of delivery.

6. Order ceilings

Putting in place order thresholds entails providing free shipping for purchases over a predetermined amount. Customers are encouraged to add more goods to their cart in order to meet the requirement, which could balance shipping costs with higher average order values. An excellent illustration is an online bookshop that offers free shipping on purchases above $50. In order to take advantage of the free shipping, customers are more inclined to purchase extra books.

Strategic planning requires constant monitoring and modifications

It is not a one-time project. To make sure your initiatives are still successful in lowering delivery costs while upholding customer satisfaction, regularly examine your shipment data, carrier partnerships, and consumer feedback.

1.Logistics Improvement

Making informed judgments about carrier selection, fulfillment strategies, and continual improvements are necessary for effective logistics optimization. This strategy guarantees effective shipping procedures that result in lower costs. Let's examine each approach in more detail:

Selection and negotiation of the carrier
It's critical to pick the best shipping company for your needs. Look into and contrast different carriers based on things like shipment costs, turnaround times, and dependability. Negotiate with carriers to get lower prices based on the volume and frequency of your shipments. For instance, a handcrafted jewelry internet store can bargain with shipping companies to get lower costs for its delicate and lightweight items.

2. Comparison of shipping choices

Find the most affordable and appropriate shipping alternatives for the various sorts of shipments by carefully comparing all available options. Take into account elements like shipping costs, monitoring availability, and delivery time. You can compare shipping prices between carriers using online shipping calculators. Consider a retailer of online toys who offers both standard and expedited shipment. They can discover when comparing carriers that one offers reasonable costs for standard shipping while another is better for expedited orders.

3. Fulfillment by a third party

Third-party fulfillment entails contracting with a specialized company to handle your order processing, warehousing, and delivery. These suppliers frequently have established connections with carriers, giving you access to lower delivery costs. An organization that sells beauty boxes by subscription, for instance, might collaborate with a different fulfillment facility. In addition to streamlining their processes, this gives them access to discounted shipping rates, which lowers the entire cost of shipping.

4. Constant development

Every great company is built on a culture of constant development. It entails evaluating and optimizing your shipping procedures on a regular basis. Track carrier performance, get client feedback, and spot areas that could use improvement. An online furniture company, for instance, might discover that clients in particular areas routinely have shipping delays. They can raise consumer satisfaction by dealing with these problems and perhaps even bargain better shipping conditions with carriers.

By optimizing your shipping procedures and ensuring that you are obtaining the best value for your shipping fees, each logistics optimization strategy helps to reduce costs. Keep in mind that logistics optimization is a continuous process that calls for flexibility and a readiness to change in response to shifting market conditions and consumer expectations.

Chapter 14

Using data analytics to track the success of your online store

Data analytics is a potent instrument that can aid in the optimization of your e-commerce marketing campaigns. You may learn more about your customers, test and improve your campaigns, track and analyze your outcomes, discover and put into effect best practices, and predict and foresee future trends by employing data analytics.

1. Recognize your audience

You can segment your consumer base using data analytics, taking into account their feedback, behavior, preferences, and demographics. You can monitor and measure your customers' actions, such as browsing, clicking, adding items to carts, making purchases, or abandoning carts, using data analytics solutions like Google Analytics, Facebook Pixel, or Shopify Analytics. Knowing the needs, wants, and pain points of your clients can help you develop unique, pertinent marketing messages that will appeal to them and encourage them to make a purchase.

2. Evaluate and improve your marketing

By comparing various factors, such as headlines, graphics, copy, offers, channels, or audiences, data analytics can assist you in testing and optimizing your marketing efforts. To determine which version of your campaign performs better in terms of conversions, income, or engagement, you may run A/B testing or multivariate tests using data analytics tools like Google Optimize, Unbounce, or Mailchimp. You may raise your return on investment (ROI) and lower your cost per acquisition (CPA) by experimenting with and fine-tuning your campaigns.

3. Monitor and assess your outcomes

By monitoring and reporting your key performance indicators (KPIs), such as traffic, leads, sales, retention, or loyalty, data analytics may help you assess and evaluate your results. To generate dashboards and visualizations that demonstrate your progress and impact, you can utilize data analytics tools like Google Data Studio, Tableau, or Power BI. You can determine your strengths and weaknesses, gain knowledge from your triumphs and mistakes, and modify your strategy as necessary by measuring and assessing your results.

4. Discover and use excellent practices

By comparing your performance to that of your rivals, industry norms, or best practices, data analytics can assist you in learning and implementing best practices.

To learn more about and evaluate the strategies, practices, and outcomes of your competitors, use data analytics tools like SEMrush, Moz, or BuzzSumo. To access and learn from the most recent e-commerce marketing trends, strategies, and case studies, use data analytics tools like those offered by HubSpot, Neil Patel, or MarketingProfs. You may innovate your marketing efforts and stay on top of the game by studying and putting best practices into practice.

5. Foresee and predict future tendencies

By utilizing cutting-edge methodologies like machine learning, artificial intelligence, or natural language processing, data analytics can assist you in anticipating and predicting future trends. You may create and train models that can estimate demand, promote items, produce content, or optimize pricing using data analytics tools like IBM Watson, Google Cloud AI, or Amazon SageMaker. You can adjust to shifting customer expectations and market conditions and gain a competitive edge by predicting and anticipating future trends.

Data analytics is a potent instrument that can aid in the optimization of your e-commerce marketing campaigns. You may learn more about your customers, test and improve your campaigns, track and analyze your outcomes, discover and put into effect best practices, and predict and foresee future trends by employing data analytics.

By doing so, you can increase your customer satisfaction, loyalty, and retention, and ultimately grow your e-commerce business.

Chapter 15

Encourage client feedback and gather it to make required adjustments and foster confidence.

If you operate your own company, I'm sure you go above and beyond to win over clients, meet their demands, and maintain their brand loyalty. However, how can you be certain that your efforts will have the desired impact? You will never be able to provide your customers with the ideal experience if you do not make an effort to learn what they think about your service. You can use their feedback on their interactions with your brand to improve your company and better cater to their demands.

There are numerous ways to capitalize on client comments and make money. In this article, I'll discuss why getting consumer feedback, whether requested or uninvited, is essential for managing client satisfaction and loyalty, retaining clients, enhancing goods and services, and many other aspects of your company.

Pay attention and feel what they are saying.

Listening and showing empathy are the first steps in handling client comments and concerns. Don't disregard, ignore, or dispute with your clients. Instead, be mindful of their emotions, apologize for any difficulty, and express gratitude for their suggestions. Show them your concern and willingness to assist. Avoid jargon and prefabricated responses, and speak in a kind and cheerful manner. Building rapport and relieving tension can be accomplished by listening and empathizing.

Learn and develop

Utilizing feedback and complaints from customers to learn from them is the last phase. Don't be defensive or take them personally. As an alternative, examine them to find patterns, trends, and underlying reasons. Utilize them to enhance your communication, procedures, policies, goods, and services. Implement adjustments, then gauge the impact. Re-ask for input to determine whether the problem has been fixed or improved. Enhancing customer loyalty through learning and improvement can demonstrate your dedication and responsiveness.

Promote and honor

Encouragement and reward are proactive ways to address client comments and complaints. Don't wait for your customers to get in touch with you or voice their displeasure. Invite them to talk to you about their thoughts, ideas, or experiences instead. Use surveys, reviews, testimonials, or social media to collect feedback. Provide incentives, discounts, freebies, or loyalty points to reward your customers for their feedback. Encouraging and rewarding can increase customer engagement and retention and generate positive word-of-mouth.

Showcase and celebrate

Another way to handle customer feedback and complaints is to showcase and celebrate them. Don't hide or delete them from your website or social media. Instead, display them proudly and publicly. Highlight your positive feedback and testimonials and show how you value your customers. Respond to your negative feedback and complaints and show how you handle them effectively and professionally. Showcase and celebration can boost your credibility and reputation and attract new customers.

Use social media, questionnaires, reviews, or other methods to gather customer feedback. Incentives, discounts, gifts, or loyalty points can be given as a way to thank your consumers for their input. Encouragement and rewards can boost customer engagement, retention, and word-of-mouth recommendations.

Showcase and enjoy

Showcase and appreciate client feedback and grievances as an additional means of handling them. Don't remove or hide them from your social media or website. Instead, flaunt them in front of others. Showcase your satisfied clients' comments and recommendations to demonstrate how much you value them. Respond to concerns and negative feedback, and demonstrate how you handle them skillfully and professionally. Showcase and celebration can improve your brand and credibility and draw in new clients.

Track and quantify

Monitoring and measuring client comments and complaints is the final approach. Once you've dealt with them, don't disregard or forget about them. Instead, consistently and methodically track and analyze them. Measure your customer happiness, loyalty, retention, churn, and advocacy using metrics, tools, or software. Compare your performance against your targets, industry standards, or rivals. You may analyze your progress and pinpoint areas for improvement by using monitor and measure.

Chapter 16

Adding new markets and product lines

You may build brand awareness and generate buzz for your company when you enter new markets and interact with new clients. As consumers become more familiar with your brand and what you have to offer as a result of this raised awareness, you may see a rise in sales and profits. Expanding your product line has numerous advantages, including the potential to significantly increase overall market demand.

There are numerous ways to broaden your product offering. For instance, you may expand your existing selection to include more colors, sizes, and styles. If you're selling internationally, you could also wish to customize your product selection according to the nation.

Additionally, it's a simple approach to draw in more customers and make the most of your current audience.
Modern shoppers prefer convenience and simplicity when buying. Expanding your product mix will enable you to offer clients more and better options, improving the likelihood that you can meet their needs.

Let's first examine a few of the factors that leading online retailers are using to expand their product lines.

An important tactic for increasing sales is cultivating a following of devoted clients because it is typically less expensive than acquiring new clients.

By expanding your product offering, you may provide your clients more choices. They won't feel compelled to visit your competitors' websites if they can discover what they require on your sales channels.

AOV (Average Order Value) growth is a typical KPI in the eCommerce industry. You want to get the most out of a visitor that is looking at your stuff. A quick and low-cost approach to do that is to raise your AOV.

Here, the focus is on product sets and bundles. By establishing product relationships, you may show customers products that are pertinent to and related to the one they are viewing. The potential for creating kits and bundles increases as you increase the number of products you provide.

By adding more kits and bundles, you may expand the selection of already popular products. Giving your consumers this extra option will probably persuade them to fill their baskets with more items. When illustrating the relationships between products, you can adopt an educational stance. Make sure your language conveys that they are being informed of the other complementary products available.

Making the most of long tailing is becoming simpler with the rising popularity of techniques like drop shipping. Here, you can sell less quantities of difficult-to-find goods while earning higher profit margins.

Your catalog will get a competitive edge and improve your online positioning if you include these specialty products. Customers will value the ability to locate products that are difficult to discover.

You may distinguish yourself from the rest of your rivals by providing these specialized products. You'll probably see increased client loyalty in addition to By providing upselling chances with the least amount of investment, you can enhance your sales.

Many of the dangers and difficulties associated with traditional eCommerce and distribution are removed by dropshipping. You've made investments in your brand, and your consumer base is expanding and devoted. By dropshipping from your dependable supply chain, you may improve the experience you provide for your clients and increase your revenue.

By using dropshipping, you may sell the products of your suppliers and have them send them right to your clients. This means that it avoids passing through your warehouse, which results in significant cost savings on pricey real estate and logistics. Which products from your suppliers go on your sales channels is entirely up to you. The assets can then be improved with your brand's style and voice in mind.

Only after a customer places an online order will the product be added to your ERP via your PIM. Your interconnected systems won't, therefore, be burdened until absolutely essential.

You can extend your target market and increase your consumer base by adding more products to your range of offerings. At this point, you might want to think about offering many product variations at a range of price points. This minimizes the possibility of losing clients due to pricing choices.

By doing this, you can target a wide range of demographics and meet the specific requirements of your clients. Your brand's reach will grow if you sell goods at various price points, which will also make purchasing more accessible.

Increase the likelihood of upselling by delivering superior products with ease. Retailers who develop budget or plus size lines, for instance, are also serving a bigger target market.

Chapter 17

Keep up with business changes and technological developments

You can use these techniques to stay current with e-commerce business changes and technical advancements. Read industry blogs and e-commerce news websites frequently. The most recent trends and developments are frequently covered on websites like TechCrunch, E-commerce Times, and industry-specific blogs.

Follow e-commerce thought leaders, business pioneers, and pertinent hashtags on social media sites like Twitter and LinkedIn. This may offer current information and perspectives. Attend e-commerce seminars, webinars, and conferences. Exporto frequently discuss the most recent developments and tactics at these events.

Enroll in e-commerce and technology-related online courses or programs. Relevant courses are available on websites like Coursera, edX, and LinkedIn Learning. Join e-commerce forums and communities like r/ecommerce on Reddit, BigCommerce Community, or Shopify Community. Participating in discussions might aid in keeping you updated.

During your commute or free time, listen to podcasts about e-commerce and technology. Industry experts frequently share their knowledge and experiences in podcasts. Join industry associations, thought leaders, and companies that provide e-commerce technology newsletters and email updates. These newsletters frequently include insightful information and updates.

To meet people in the e-commerce industry, go to networking events both offline and online. By using unofficial methods, networking can help you keep informed. Watch out for your rivals. Examine their websites, business plans, and technology use to spot trends and advances.

Make it a habit to learn. Set aside some time each week to investigate and examine e-commerce trends and new technology. You will be better able to adapt to change as a result of this continual effort. Consider taking part in e-commerce platforms or technology beta testing initiatives. By doing so, you may have early access to new features and knowledge of their possible effects.

Encourage client feedback and keep an eye on client testimonials. Customers frequently have valuable insights into your ecommerce business's strengths and areas for improvement. Combining these tactics will help you keep up with how e-commerce is changing.